GCSE 9–1
ANIMAL FARM
BY GEORGE ORWELL
GREAT ANSWERS

SCHOLASTIC

Published in the UK by Scholastic Education, 2020

Book End, Range Road, Witney, Oxfordshire, OX29 0YD

A division of Scholastic Limited

London – New York – Toronto – Sydney – Auckland

Mexico City – New Delhi – Hong Kong

SCHOLASTIC and associated logos are trademarks and/or registered trademarks of Scholastic Inc.

www.scholastic.co.uk

1 2 3 4 5 6 7 8 9   0 1 2 3 4 5 6 7 8 9

British Library Cataloguing-in-Publication Data

A catalogue record for this book is available from the British Library.

ISBN 978-1407-18399-2

Printed and bound by Bell and Bain Ltd, Glasgow

Papers used by Scholastic Limited are made from wood grown in sustainable forests.

Author

Richard Durant

Editorial team

Audrey Stokes, Vicki Yates, Kate Pedlar, Julia Roberts

Typesetting

Jayne Rawlings/Oxford Raw Design

Design team

Dipa Mistry

Illustration

Rosalia Ra.Ro Radosti

Contents

About this book

This book is designed to demonstrate what a great answer for your AQA GCSE English Literature exam question on *Animal Farm* (Paper 2, Section A) looks like. It demonstrates a step-by-step process from first sight of the question through to a full answer. This process shows you how to approach each step, from analysing what the question is asking you to do, to planning your answer, showing how it meets the assessment objectives for the exam paper and finally presenting a great answer and an examiner's response. All the answers in this book have been written in the light of advice from examiners and using tips drawn from the examiners' reports over the last few years.

It is important to note that one question can give rise to multiple different great answers. What these great answers all have in common is that they are based on an excellent interpretation with sound exploration of evidence. Great answers are not *right* answers, they are rich and well-argued answers.

In this book you will find the following features that will help you understand how to achieve that all-important great answer in your exam.

Zoom in on the question

How does Orwell use events in *Animal Farm* to explore ideas about the consequences of rebellion?

Write about:

- some of the events in the novel
- how Orwell uses these events to explore ideas about the consequences of rebellion.

Concentrate on Orwell's purposes, referring to events/themes in the novel as a whole to address. (AO1)

Stay relevant to the question focus. Consider how Orwell organises his plot to emphasise consequences. (AO2)

Refer to Orwell's choice of words and **structure** to emphasise his ideas. (AO2)

Consider how Orwell's ideas and methods might be influenced by his beliefs and experiences. (AO3)

Analysis of the question to help you focus on what the question is actually asking you.

Ideas to help you cover the AOs for each question and matching colour-coded commentary within the answers to show you how these are achieved.

AO1
Evaluate Orwell's possible intentions in writing an **allegory**/fairy story. Consider alternative interpretations: warning or pure pessimism? Identify three main consequences of the revolution: the animals' pride; failure to check the pigs' power; the rebellion's 'mythology' (the building of a shared 'myth' or legend of the first rebellion, which binds them together).

AO2
How does Orwell's tone and language support his intentions? Note the significance of the traditional fairy-tale genre. How does Orwell sequence events to emphasise the tragedy of the rebellion's consequences?

AO3
Note the significance of the novel's subtitle ('A Fairy Story'); consider how what we know about Orwell's life and beliefs sheds light on his intentions.

elections, and even, in part, the presence of oppressive regimes throughout history[4]. This attitude might well make Orwell's message of acceptance and helplessness more familiar and acceptable, and he never gives any hope to the reader that Napoleon's greed and wickedness will be checked – even Benjamin (representing the intellectuals), who quickly recognises that Napoleon's leadership is no better than that of Jones, is too cynical, or accepting, to take action. The rest of the animals' misery and poverty gets worse and worse, as each of the commandments (the basis of a fair society under Animalism) is undone[5], and when they get a chance to turn on the pigs, even Boxer, a model of honesty and goodness, absurdly blames himself for not working hard enough. The plot of *Animal Farm* gives no relief to this sense of the animals' headlong collapse into misery and degradation, a collapse explained by the basic failings of human nature – either selfishness (the pigs) or stupidity (the other animals)[6].

[4] AO1/AO3: Orwell's views helpfully put in context of ideas generally held by people.

[5] AO2: insights into relentless plot structure and how this reinforces sense of pessimism.

Paragraph	Content		Timing
1	Intro – use the question prep to establish focus of answer, and question whether Orwell is against all leaders.		9.40
2	Napoleon's leadership characteristics.	Refer back to question focus sometimes. Question Orwell's attitude to leadership. Analyse some examples of his word choices.	9.43
3	Snowball's leadership characteristics.		9.56
4	Boxer's leadership characteristics.		10.09
5	Conclusion – brief return to question/distinction between leaders and leadership/how Orwell's own views might be evident in the novel.		10.22

Essay plans and timings to help you plan more efficiently.

DO IT!

Now use what you have learned to answer the following AQA exam-style question.

How does Orwell use events in *Animal Farm* to explore ideas about trust and loyalty?

Write about:

- some of the events in the novel
- how Orwell uses these events to explore ideas about trust and loyalty.

[30 marks]
AO4 [4 marks]

Exam-style questions using previously unseen text extracts, allowing you to put into practice the skills you've learned and create a great answer by yourself.

AQA exam-style questions using the *same* extract provided for the Great Answer analysis which precedes it.

Online answers

Designed to guide you towards structuring a really 'great answer' and consolidate your understanding through thought and application (including an AO breakdown). Remember: it is important to write your own answers before checking online at **www.scholastic.co.uk/gcse.**

Advice for students

✓ **Know your text well.** This will help you to demonstrate your knowledge and understanding in the exam. Concentrate on knowing the text well rather than predicting questions.

✓ **Read the question carefully and answer the question.** Be sure you are answering the question you have chosen and *not* the one that you would have preferred to see on the paper.

✓ **Take time to think about and plan your answer.** Gathering your thoughts will give you space to address the question and choose appropriate references and details to support and develop your answer.

✓ **Demonstrate your knowledge by referencing parts of the play.** But make sure it is relevant, you don't get extra marks for more quotations, but you do get more marks for making interesting comments about the references you have selected.

✓ **Read the extracts very carefully.** It is helpful to place the extract in the **context** of the play – at what point, what happened before and/or after, which characters are involved, how does it link to other parts of the text. Be sure that you understand the meaning and context of quotations you choose from the extract.

✓ **Recognise that 'writer's methods' means anything the writer has done deliberately.** This covers the writer's use of language and techniques, the **structure** of the text and characterisation.

✓ **Understand the connection between the writer's methods and the writer's ideas.** It might be helpful to think about *how* the writer does something and *why* the writer does something.

✓ **Link comments on contextual factors/ideas to the text.** Keep in mind that context informs but should never dominate your reading of the text; the text comes first. Relating the extract to the whole text is a valid approach to context.

Question 1

How does Orwell use events in *Animal Farm* to explore ideas about the consequences of rebellion?

Write about:

*   some of the events in the novel

*   how Orwell uses these events to explore ideas about the consequences of rebellion.

[30 marks]
AO4 [4 marks]

Zoom in on the question

How does Orwell use events in *Animal Farm* to explore ideas about the consequences of rebellion?

Write about:

*   some of the events in the novel
*   how Orwell uses these events to explore ideas about the consequences of rebellion.

Concentrate on Orwell's purposes, referring to events/themes in the novel as a whole to address. (AO1)

Stay relevant to the question focus. Consider how Orwell organises his plot to emphasise consequences. (AO2)

Refer to Orwell's choice of words and **structure** to emphasise his ideas. (AO2)

Consider how Orwell's ideas and methods might be influenced by his beliefs and experiences. (AO3)

Here are some ideas that could be included in an answer in order to cover the Assessment Objectives (AOs).

AO1

Evaluate Orwell's possible intentions in writing an **allegory**/fairy story. Consider alternative interpretations: warning or pure pessimism? Identify three main consequences of the revolution: the animals' pride; failure to check the pigs' power; the rebellion's 'mythology' (the building of a shared 'myth' or legend of the first rebellion, which binds them together).

AO2

How does Orwell's tone and language support his intentions? Note the significance of the traditional fairy-tale genre. How does Orwell sequence events to emphasise the tragedy of the rebellion's consequences?

AO3

Note the significance of the novel's subtitle ('A Fairy Story'); consider how what we know about Orwell's life and beliefs sheds light on his intentions.

A student has decided to focus on whether or not Orwell is suggesting that the consequences are inevitable. This is the plan they have made to answer the question.

Paragraph	Content		Timing
1	Intro – use the question prep to establish focus of answer, and my key question above: pure pessimism or warning?		9.40
2	Consequence 1: animals' lives are at first enriched by a sense of dignity, pride, independence.	Refer back to question focus sometimes. Consider Orwell's intentions, structure, language choices.	9.43
3	Consequence 2: animals entrust pigs with power.		9.56
4	Consequence 3: pigs exploit shared mythology created by the rebellion.		10.09
5	Conclusion – brief return to pessimism/warning. Refer to novel's 'fairy tale' subtitle.		10.22

The essay plan above will meet these Assessment Objectives:

AO1 Read, understand and respond	Interpret Orwell's 'message' and his intentions through consideration of three important consequences of the rebellion. Support this analysis with specific references to the novel.
AO2 Language, form and structure	Identify the impact of word choices, plot events, how the plot is organised and the significance of allegory and fairy tale.
AO3 Contexts	Consider how aspects of Orwell's life and beliefs, and typical elements of traditional fairy tales, shed light on Orwell's intentions.

You could read *Animal Farm* as a pessimistic warning by George Orwell that rebellion is doomed to failure and that the consequences of rebellion[1] are worse than not rebelling at all. Perhaps he was suggesting[2] that rebellion ends up by giving power to those who are even worse than the ones overthrown by the rebellion. However, despite what happens in the novel[1], Orwell is probably not advising people to tolerate a life of servitude, or misery, rather than rebel. After all, Orwell was a socialist who passionately wrote and spoke against poverty and exploitation, and who risked his life to fight against fascism in the Spanish Civil War[3]. More likely[2], *Animal Farm* warns about the sort of negative consequences of revolution that Orwell saw in the Russian Revolution and the rise of Stalin's dictatorship. Orwell wrote his *Animal Farm* allegory to warn future revolutionaries against making the same mistakes[3].

The positive consequence of rebellion[4] is that at first the animals have a motivating and powerful sense of dignity and pride: they are 'their own masters'. This pride sustains them through events that otherwise would be crippling. Orwell deliberately creates desperate events to emphasise[5] the strength of the animals' new sense of pride: eg they have to build their windmill three times, and with very little food to fuel their efforts[6]. They also have to bravely withstand two invasions of the farm by armed and murderous humans. Orwell shows how the pigs turn the animals' new-found optimism against them: cynically, Squealer reassures the animals that although they have lost everything to the pigs, they are still 'their own masters'[6], working for their own benefit. However bad things are now, they are better than before.

That is what is so tragic in the novel[7]: Orwell ensures that[5] every new misfortune he heaps on the animals, such as a long working week and reduced rations, is reinterpreted for them by the pigs as a victory for all animals. Once the revolution is achieved, the pigs' cunning and the immediate need for continuous and exhausting work distracts the animals from another consequence of the rebellion – the need to maintain the equality, democracy and collaborative effort[7] that made the initial overthrow of the humans possible. Instead, the animals hand their power over to the pigs and allow them to rule for them. The result is devastating, but it is also farcical and funny in a terrible way[8]. This is particularly true of the second invasion, which results in the second destruction of the windmill and the deaths of some animals. The animals are depressed but Orwell has Squealer 'come skipping' up to announce a great victory worth celebrating. The verb 'skipping' emphasises Squealer's – and the pigs' – insensitivity and selfishness, but is also comically incongruous with the other animals' misery[9].

1 AO1: clear opening, using words and ideas from the question to ensure relevance.

2 AO1/AO3: 'conceptual' approach – question focus viewed in terms of two possible sorts of warning.

3 AO3: Orwell's intentions usefully considered in the **context** of his beliefs and contemporary political events.

4 AO1: words from the question 'anchor' the paragraph to relevant focus.

5 AO1: clear understanding of Orwell's deliberate intentions.

6 AO1: deft, relevant use of both indirect references and quotation to illustrate points.

7 AO1: paragraph introduces and explores specific, relevant aspect of question focus – the consequence of entrusting the pigs with power.

8 AO2: clear appreciation of **effect** of one structural feature – tragic comedy/farce.

9 AO1/AO2: apt quotation explored for its subtle effects.

Squealer's behaviour here[10] is typical of the pigs' brazenness: their behaviour and announcements clearly contradict the original principles of 'animalism', but each contradiction is justified by a warped appeal to the values and the mythology of the early days of the rebellion against the humans. Orwell makes sure that each contradiction – sleeping in beds, savagely executing animals, collaborating with humans – is more shocking than the last[11]. His point is that one consequence of rebellion is that it gives the animals a shared narrative and set of values – a shared 'mythology' – that the pigs can exploit to justify their excesses. Of course, the pigs do not just exploit this shared history: they rewrite it. For example, over time, Snowball develops from being the heroic defender of the revolution to the leader of the forces who try to overthrow it, and the sacred 'seven commandments' are gradually and sneakily revised[12].

Animal Farm is subtitled 'A Fairy Story', a genre which traditionally teaches an important lesson through a simple story; Orwell's 'fairy story' is an allegory[13], a simple retelling of the events of the Russian Revolution and how this was corrupted. With this in mind, it seems unlikely that the lesson of Orwell's fairy tale is to tolerate miserable conditions. Instead, the lesson is to understand the possible unintended consequences of a rebellion so that they can hopefully be avoided[14].

[10] AO1: this paragraph – like the last – links well to the previous paragraph, thus developing the core argument in the answer.

[11] AO2: insight into how Orwell *develops* our understanding of the consequences of rebellion (structure).

[12] AO1: excellent choice of references to support the 'point'.

[13] AO2: precise and useful **subject-specific terminology**.

[14] AO1/AO3: sharp understanding of 'fairy tale' genre leads to deeper appreciation of aspects of Orwell's intentions.

Commentary

This is an intelligent, enquiring response that presents and explores a well-developed argument. It takes a conceptualised approach to the question focus, exploring evidence for Orwell's intentions. Precisely chosen references and **subject-specific terminology** support the analysis. Connotations of Orwell's words and how these reveal his intentions are deftly explored. The answer is full of perceptive insights that are woven into a convincing argument.

DOIT!

Now use what you have learned to answer the following AQA exam-style question.

How does Orwell use events in *Animal Farm* to explore ideas about trust and loyalty?

Write about:

- some of the events in the novel
- how Orwell uses these events to explore ideas about trust and loyalty.

[30 marks]
AO4 [4 marks]

Question 2

How does Orwell use Boxer and Benjamin to explore attitudes to revolution in *Animal Farm*?

Write about:

- what Boxer and Benjamin say and do

- how Orwell uses Boxer and Benjamin to explore attitudes to revolution.

[30 marks]
AO4 [4 marks]

Concentrate on Orwell's purposes, referring to events/themes in the novel as a whole to address AO1. Stay relevant to the question focus: how Orwell uses Boxer and Benjamin to explore attitudes to revolution.

Zoom in on the question

How does Orwell use Boxer and Benjamin to explore attitudes to revolution in *Animal Farm*?

Write about:

- what Boxer and Benjamin say and do

- how Orwell uses Boxer and Benjamin to explore attitudes to revolution.

Look for evidence to support points in what characters *say* and do. (AO1/AO2)

Refer to Orwell's choice of words and structure to emphasise his ideas. (AO2)

Explore the novel's message about the real world in Orwell's time. (AO3)

Here are some ideas that could be included in an answer in order to cover the Assessment Objectives (AOs).

AO1	AO2	AO3
Note the differences in the presentation of Boxer and Benjamin, including 'personalities', beliefs, physical depiction and how they react to events. Consider how sympathetic each **character** appears, how Boxer is respected by Benjamin and how Benjamin's respect reinforces *our* respect for Boxer.	Explore how Orwell structures the plot: Boxer's naivety becomes more obvious; Benjamin's scepticism becomes more valid. How does Orwell use language and the 'fairy story' genre to guide reader reactions and suggest Orwell's own views?	Consider what Boxer and Benjamin **represent** in the context of the Russian Revolution (hard-working, loyal but unquestioning workers; intellectuals who perhaps didn't do enough to halt the rise of Stalin).

A student has decided to focus on contrast between the characters and how they might be seen as complementary. This is the plan they have made to answer the question.

Paragraph	Content		Timing
1	Intro – use the question prep to establish focus of answer, and my key idea.		9.40
2	Boxer's admirable strengths and how these are used against him.	Refer back to question focus sometimes. Question what Orwell might be suggesting about revolution/what readers' attitudes might be.	9.43
3	Benjamin – positive and negative. Explore his response to destruction of windmill.		9.56
4	Return to Boxer. Contrasts with Benjamin. How a reader is likely to react to his blind faith.		10.09
5	Conclusion – brief return to question/make explicit suggestion about Orwell's intentions.		10.22

The essay plan above will meet these Assessment Objectives:

AO1 Read, understand and respond	Give an interpretation of Benjamin and Boxer and analysis of Orwell's purposes. Summarise the two characters' essential **characteristics**, how these contrast and how they might both contribute to Orwell's concerns.
AO2 Language, form and structure	Analyse the effect on the reader of examples of what Boxer and Benjamin say and do. Explore how the ending emphasises Boxer's folly/pigs' callousness.
AO3 Contexts	Explain the significance of 'fairy story' aspects suggested by the novel's subtitle.

Orwell uses Boxer and Benjamin to explore contrasting – and in some ways complementary[1] – attitudes towards revolution[2]. Boxer remains positive and optimistic[3] throughout the novel despite the mounting hardships, his own injuries and exhaustion and the pigs' treachery. Benjamin, on the other hand[3], is suspicious and sceptical, and he refuses to work any harder than is good for him. Boxer may be regarded as symbolic of the working classes after the Russian Revolution – loyal and hard-working but perhaps naive and unquestioning; Benjamin may be seen as representative of the intellectuals, who were more cynical during Stalin's rise to power but, arguably, did not do enough to stop it[4]. Orwell presents both Boxer and Benjamin sympathetically, suggesting he understands the position of both[1].

For his part in the Battle of the Cowshed, Boxer is honoured with an 'Animal Hero First Class'[5] medal, and for all the animals, as well as the reader[6], he is a real hero. In the years after the overthrow of Jones, he makes sure that the revolution survives by leading by example. He works very hard, despite his tiredness and lack of food. No setback destroys his optimism or his belief that anything can be achieved through hard work. In fact, at the lowest point, when they are having to rebuild the windmill, the animals get 'more inspiration'[5] from Boxer's strength and determination than from Squealer's motivational speeches. Added to Boxer's strength, determination and selflessness is his blind trust, expressed in his slogan 'Napoleon is always right'[5]. The animals admire and respect Boxer, and so Orwell most likely intended the reader to do so too[6]. However, his unquestioning loyalty undermines his admirable strengths, and he ends up sold to the knacker's yard, his purchase price converted into a case of whisky[7].

In Benjamin, Orwell creates a quite different collection of qualities. Benjamin is small but he is also fierce: he is 'the worst tempered' animal on the farm. Instead of automatically trusting authority he is naturally suspicious. He doesn't trust the pigs' motives and sees through their lies and propaganda; he is the one who warns Boxer that he is being betrayed by the pigs. Despite being left 'quite unchanged' by the revolution, he risks his life to defend it, fighting bravely and fiercely against the invasion. Overall, Benjamin is a sympathetic character[8]. Unlike Boxer, he is cautious and not naively positive. Instead he is a fatalist who believes that life will always go 'badly'. Orwell does not fully endorse Benjamin's cynical, detached attitude[8]. When humans are preparing to blow up the windmill, we sense that Benjamin gets a perverse satisfaction out of correctly predicting the calamity. Benjamin watches with 'an air almost of amusement'. Here Benjamin is not just being realistic; he is almost

[1] AO1: 'conceptual' approach – the 'complementary' roles of Benjamin and Boxer.

[2] AO1: clear opening, using words from the question to ensure relevance.

[3] AO1: deft summary of main differences between the two characters.

[4] AO3: novel set usefully in context of Russian Revolution.

[5] AO1: precise and accurate use of quotation.

[6] AO1: perceptive reference to how Orwell builds the *reader's* attitudes and sympathies. Insight into *Orwell's purposes*.

[7] AO2: paragraph provides insight into how Orwell *develops* our understanding of his themes through plot development (structure).

[8] AO1: an exploratory response and sensitivity to the subtleties of Benjamin's character lead to insights into how Orwell is using Benjamin to make a political point.

revelling in misery and disaster. Orwell must have known the word 'amusement' might almost offend the reader[9].

In addition to Boxer's physical strength, Orwell emphasises his gentleness and sensitivity to others. This is shown right at the start of the novel when he and Clover come into Major's meeting in the barn, taking 'great care' not to tread on any small animals in the hay. However, Orwell shows Boxer's sensitivity and trust to be his downfall; his motto that 'Napoleon is always right'[9] is surely ironic. Boxer's blind faith in the revolution's self-appointed leaders makes him banish any doubts he has about the pigs' behaviour. He even fails to recognise that Napoleon has deliberately set the dogs on him[10].

Orwell suggests that both Benjamin's and Boxer's attitudes are valuable and even admirable, but they are not enough on their own. Benjamin's cryptic declaration that 'Donkeys live a long time' means that donkeys see lots of changes, but everything really always remains the same. Orwell makes this idea dramatically true at the end of the novel when the animals are no longer able to see a difference between the pigs and the humans. Orwell himself is probably not a cynic like Benjamin. Instead, *Animal Farm* could be read as a warning – that a revolution can only survive if the participants combine the best of both Benjamin and Boxer[11]; that perhaps if the Russian Revolutionaries of 1917 had been less naive, with some of Benjamin's cautionary cynicism, they may have been able to avoid the unintended outcome of decades under Stalin's dictatorship.

[9] **AO2:** clear understanding of how Orwell chooses language for meaning and effect.

[10] **AO1:** useful development of analysis of how Orwell uses contradiction and contrast to make his points.

[11] **AO1:** clear and perceptive conclusion that reinforces the answer's central point about how Benjamin and Boxer complement each other within Orwell's purposes.

Commentary

This answer is thoughtful, exploratory and very effectively structured to make the central argument convincing. The answer holds to a clear and specific concept – how Benjamin and Boxer both contrast and complement each other – and this is well supported by a range of precise references to the text. The answer shows a sophisticated appreciation of how language and form contribute to Orwell's purposes, and overall the answer demonstrates a clear insight into how Orwell deliberately makes choices of character, language and form to develop meaning and effect.

DO IT!

Now use what you have learned to answer the following AQA exam-style question.

How does Orwell use Snowball and Napoleon to explore attitudes to revolution in *Animal Farm*?

Write about:

- what Snowball and Napoleon say and do
- how Orwell uses Snowball and Napoleon to explore attitudes to revolution.

[30 marks]
AO4 [4 marks]

Question 3

How does Orwell present the significance of Major's speech in *Animal Farm*?

Write about:

- the consequences of Major's speech

- how Orwell presents the significance of Major's speech.

[30 marks]
AO4 [4 marks]

Zoom in on the question

> Notice what Orwell does deliberately. (AO1)

How does Orwell present the significance of Major's speech in *Animal Farm*?

Write about:

- the consequences of Major's speech

- how Orwell presents the significance of Major's speech.

> Stay relevant to the question focus. Consider how Orwell present the significance of Major's speech. (AO1/AO2)

> What are Orwell's attitude and his methods (choice of words and structure)? (AO2)

> Consider Orwell's attitudes in light of events in Orwell's own life and times to address AO3.

Here are some ideas that could be included in an answer so as to cover the Assessment Objectives (AOs).

AO1
What is Orwell suggesting about Major's ideals? Explore how the pigs exploit the speech for their own purposes and the purpose of the speech as a dramatic launching point for the novel's events.

AO2
Discuss how the novel's structure leads out of Major's speech and turns it on its head; include examples of **irony** and **euphemism**.

AO3
Explore the consequences for all of us – and/or the people of post-revolution Russia – of the principles promoted by Major. Consider the role of inspiring speeches in general. Is inspiration enough? What is the difference between Major's 'vision' (an idea of a better future for all the animals) and the pigs' propaganda (the twisting of the truth to make the animals believe that they are living Major's vision)?

A student has decided to focus on the 'bitter irony' of Major's principles when taken over by the pigs. This is the plan they have made to answer the question.

Paragraph	Content		Timing
1	Intro – use the question prep to establish focus of answer: specific consequences (dramatic, political, ironic).		9.40
2	Circular plot in which, ironically, Major's principles are inverted by the pigs: the habits that Major criticised Jones for are adopted by the pigs. The end completes the circle, and the animals are in the same, if not worse, position than they were at the start, just with someone else in charge.	Refer back to question focus sometimes. Consider evidence. Question Orwell's intentions.	9.43
3	Specific aspect of pigs' betrayal (taking the milk and apples, drinking whisky): pigs' ingratitude towards other animals.		9.56
4	Significance of violence suggested by Major's rebellion, which **foreshadows** the escalation of violence as the novel progresses.		10.09
5	Conclusion – summarise and draw conclusions about Orwell's message for us. Include clues from Orwell's times about his views.		10.22

The essay plan above will meet these Assessment Objectives:

AO1 Read, understand and respond	Give an interpretation of Orwell's intentions: setting out an idealistic vision, which is then destroyed piece by piece, until the story comes full circle. Analyse Orwell's picture of how ideals can be warped and exploited. Consider different sorts of evidence.
AO2 Language, form and structure	Explore how the novel's structure is based on irony: Major's speech is used as a dramatic springboard.
AO3 Contexts	Discuss events in the real world that might have informed Orwell's views (Russian Revolution and its aftermath).

Major's speech is very significant in a number of ways[1]. Firstly, it is the dramatic starting point for the novel's action: the plot is an ironic unpacking of Major's speech. Secondly, the speech provides an explanation of the principles of what later becomes known as 'Animalism' and which is summarised as the 'Seven Commandments' written on the barn wall. However, a third significance is that, while the speech provides an inspiring vision of a better, fairer future, it also provides a chilling call to violence, even murder, in order to fulfil Major's aim: 'the overthrow of the human race'[2]. The pigs, of course, need no encouragement to justify the use of extreme violence.

Major's description of the misery and injustice of the animals' lives, under Jones, at the beginning of the novel, is an accurate one; it helps inspire the animals to rebel against their conditions and to overthrow Jones, in order to regain dignity and control over their own lives and the fruits of their labour. The bitter irony, though, is that Major's summary of the animals' lives under the humans' rule as 'misery and slavery' and nothing but 'hunger and overwork'[3] becomes even more true under the pigs' rule: by the end of the novel, the visiting humans congratulate the pigs on treating the animals on *Animal Farm* more harshly than the humans treated their own animals[3]. So although Major's speech is the springboard for the animals' rebellion, ironically, it leads eventually not to the animals' freedom, but to their greater enslavement. This circle of events is closed by Orwell at the end of the novel[4], when Major's words are restated in a new context with a new and bitterly ironic significance. For example[5], Major warns animals not to listen to arguments that humans and animals have shared interests; yet in their friendly meeting with the pigs at the end of the novel, Mr Pilkington asserts that there 'need not be any clash of interests whatever' between pigs and humans. Napoleon endorses this view by declaring that previous conflict between human and animals was based on a 'misunderstanding'.

Another aspect[6] of Major's condemnation of humans relates to their cruel and selfish ingratitude. He points out that, although the animals give their lives for the benefit of the humans' comfort, when the animals no longer have the strength to work, they are not rewarded but instead end up under 'the cruel knife'. Even the strongest animal, Boxer, will be callously slaughtered and boiled down to yield a final profit for the humans. Again, the bitter irony is[6] that this is actually what does happen to Boxer, except that it is the pigs and not humans who sell him to the knacker.

Of course, the pigs spend the entire novel betraying every aspect of Major's speech and his inspiring vision of a future based on fairness, freedom and equality. Even when the pigs savagely slaughter some of the

---

[1] **AO1:** clear opening, directly answering the question to ensure relevance.

[2] **AO1:** original aspect to answer – significance of violence implied in Major's 'solution'.

[3] **AO1:** deft choices of both direct and indirect references to support points.

[4] **AO2:** insight into the role of irony in the novel's structure.

[5] **AO1:** '...for example' introduces precise choices of evidence to illustrate a point.

[6] **AO1:** links to the previous paragraphs help the development of the answer's central train of thought.

animals right in front of all the other animals – in direct contradiction of Major's pronouncement that 'no animal must ever kill any other animal' – the animals do not rebel against the pigs. Perhaps the animals' reluctant acceptance of the pigs' actions is made possible by the idea of 'necessary violence' that is implied in Major's speech when he asserts that the animals must 'remove Man'. 'Removing' could be interpreted as a callous euphemism for wiping out, and when Major refers to humans as a 'race' rather than a class or just an enemy, the implications are even more chilling: Orwell would have been sharply aware of the horrors of Stalin's mass exterminations of the peasantry in Russia[7].

The plot of *Animal Farm* is a **cyclical structure**, running from Major's speech, through the pigs' warping of its principles and ending with their complete betrayal – a betrayal that Orwell emphasises by having the pigs reuse for their own benefit not just Major's principles but also his actual words[8]. The circle is so bitterly perfect that it is hard not to conclude that Orwell is suggesting that revolution may lead to something worse than the society it replaces[9]. Perhaps his idealism had been dampened by what he saw in Russia – starvation, oppression and the rise of a cruel dictator, Stalin[10]. It is likely that the failure of Major's vision reflects Orwell's disappointment when, after the 1917 revolution in Russia, one totalitarian regime was replaced by another.

[7] **AO2/AO3**: insight into the connotations of particular words for a modern reader enriched by context of the term 'ethnic cleansing', or Stalin's 'purges'.

[8] **AO1**: brief summary of evidence and ideas discussed earlier in the answer strengthens conclusion.

[9] **AO1/AO3**: consideration of Orwell's overall intentions, and the consequences for the reader.

[10] **AO3**: brief, useful consideration of the significance of Orwell's view of the rise of Stalin.

Commentary

This answer is well structured so as to develop its central insight into the role of irony in the novel's structure and its message. It takes an exploratory and critical approach that is supported by a variety of deftly chosen evidence – both analysed quotations and indirect references. The answer shows a perceptive understanding of how irony underpins the novel's structure. Subject-specific terminology (eg 'irony', 'euphemism') is deployed usefully and relevantly. The whole approach is helpfully inquiring rather than pretending to *know* what was on Orwell's mind.

DOIT!

Now use what you have learned to answer the following AQA exam-style question.

How does Orwell present the significance of the pigs' behaviour in *Animal Farm*?

Write about:

- the consequences of the pigs' behaviour
- how Orwell presents the significance of the pigs' behaviour.

[30 marks]
AO4 [4 marks]

Question 4

Boxer says 'Napoleon is always right'.

How does Orwell present leaders and leadership in *Animal Farm*?

Write about:

- what leaders say and do in the novel

- how Orwell presents leadership in the novel.

[30 marks]
AO4 [4 marks]

Zoom in on the question

Boxer says 'Napoleon is always right'.

How does Orwell present leaders and leadership in *Animal Farm*?

Write about:

- what leaders say and do in the novel

- how Orwell presents leadership in the novel.

Focus of question. Refer to Boxer and Napoleon as leaders to be analysed. (AO1)

Discuss the concept of leadership and how we understand its importance/Stalin's 'leadership' in Russia. (AO3)

Explore/analyse ideas. (AO1)

Refer to Orwell's **techniques** (for example, word choice, structure). (AO2)

Choose and analyse examples making references to the text/characters. (AO1/AO2)

Here are some ideas that could be included in an answer in order to cover the Assessment Objectives (AOs).

AO1

Analyse different leaders and the leadership characteristics they embody (for example, Snowball, Napoleon, Boxer). What does Orwell want us to conclude? Explore the tone of his presentation of leaders and leadership. Choose examples of leaders and incidents that show their leadership characteristics.

AO2

Analyse tone and how this is suggested in some word choices. Explore how Orwell develops his presentation of different types of leadership throughout the novel.

AO3

Explore Orwell's view of what constitutes a good leader/ leadership, as suggested by the novel and how Napoleon is like Stalin in Russia. Refer to Orwell's own experiences of political leadership in Spain.

A student has decided to focus on the distinction between leaders and leadership. This is the plan they have made to answer the question.

Paragraph	Content		Timing
1	Intro – use the question prep to establish focus of answer, and question whether Orwell is against all leaders.		9.40
2	Napoleon's leadership characteristics.	Refer back to question focus sometimes. Question Orwell's attitude to leadership. Analyse some examples of his word choices.	9.43
3	Snowball's leadership characteristics.		9.56
4	Boxer's leadership characteristics.		10.09
5	Conclusion – brief return to question/distinction between leaders and leadership/how Orwell's own views might be evident in the novel.		10.22

The essay plan above will meet these Assessment Objectives:

AO1 Read, understand and respond	Explore how the three leaders are presented. Consider Orwell's aims and what he wants the reader to think. Choose relevant examples and details.
AO2 Language, form and structure	Analyse the effects of some language choices. Consider the development of characters and what they represent across the whole novel.
AO3 Contexts	Refer to Orwell's own views and experiences (such as fighting in the Spanish Civil War, when many people he knew were killed as a result of Stalin's 'purges'), and how these might explain his intentions when writing.

Orwell presents different styles of leadership[1] in three very different characters – Snowball, Boxer and Napoleon. It is unclear which model of leadership Orwell himself most supports – certainly not Napoleon, but neither does he show complete support for the style of leadership shown by Snowball or Boxer. Perhaps it is not leadership, but *leaders* that Orwell is warning us against[2]. Perhaps *Animal Farm* shows us that if we let ourselves become completely dependent on any leader then progress towards what he called a 'decent society' would always collapse – as was happening in Soviet Russia (under Stalin's dictatorship, whose rise to power is depicted by that of Napoleon in the novel) and had already happened in Spain, where Orwell fought on the side of the democrats, against Franco.

Snowball is a 'decent' leader: he is brave and selfless and is genuinely committed to Major's principles and vision as expressed in 'Animalism'. As soon as Jones has been expelled, Snowball organises committees so that the animals are involved in decision-making and planning[3], showing his commitment not just to rebellion but democracy too. Then, during the Battle of the Cowshed, Snowball leads by example[3], attacking Jones's men head on, risking (and suffering) wounds for his trouble (in contrast to Napoleon later on). Even so[4], Orwell does not present Snowball as perfect: he is charismatic and inspiring, but Orwell hints that there is something shallow about him. He is 'quicker in speech' than Napoleon, but that does not prove that he is wiser and more honest than Napoleon – only that he is more persuasive. There are question marks over what Orwell calls his 'depth of character'. This **phrase** implies that Snowball has shortcomings in honesty and reliability[5].

Napoleon embodies very different leadership characteristics. He prioritises those actions that will guarantee the survival of the revolution and stop the animals from starving. He tells the animals that a 'full manger' is more important than a windmill. He also suggests that the farm should get hold of guns and learn how to use them. His outlook on the future is more practical, less inspiring than Snowball's, but at this point it does not necessarily appear to the reader to be less valid. However, Orwell makes it clear from the start[6] that Napoleon has a 'reputation for getting his own way'. In other words, for Napoleon, doing what serves his own interests is more important than fulfilling Major's dream. Napoleon is by nature a bully and an autocrat. The phrase 'getting his own way' expresses this idea in a simple, direct way that can't be missed by the reader; the colloquial style implies that the animals, too, might already recognise the bullishness of his nature[5].

1 AO1: clear opening, words from the question used to focus the answer on the question on the paper rather than the novel as a whole.

2 AO1/AO3: 'conceptual' approach – interesting distinction between leaders and leadership as a way into Orwell's intentions.

3 AO1: well-chosen indirect references to support points.

4 AO1: contradictions in Orwell's presentation helpfully signalled.

5 AO1/AO2: deft choices of quotation coupled with useful comments on significance of Orwell's language (for example, 'implies that...').

6 AO1: using Orwell's name helps to emphasise the novel as a deliberate construct with definite aims.

So, if Snowball is cunning and shallow, and Napoleon is a selfish, dishonest bully, what sort of leader is Boxer?[7] He inspires love and devotion, even from the grumpy, cynical Benjamin. Everyone admires him. When the animals' confidence hits rock bottom, it is Boxer's strength, determination and self-sacrifice that inspires them more than Squealer's propaganda. Boxer does not see himself as a leader, but he does lead by example. However, his own view of leadership, which involves handing it over to leaders – as expressed in his motto of 'Napoleon is always right' – is disastrous. If the novel is to be read as an allegory, with Boxer representing the working class, this may suggest that Orwell has a rather elitist view that the working class lack the intelligence and skill to lead well[8].

Near the end of his life, Orwell claimed that all his writing had been in favour of 'democratic socialism'. Perhaps the shortcomings shown by Napoleon, Snowball and Boxer suggest that Orwell did not trust leaders of any sort, but instead felt that it was crucial that leadership is exercised and controlled by ordinary people – 'democratic socialism' of the sort envisioned by Major. On the other hand, Orwell was sometimes accused of snobbish attitudes, so perhaps he just felt that leadership should be in the hands of 'decent, well-educated gentlemen' like himself – not honest fools like Boxer, or opportunists such as Snowball and Napoleon[9].

[7] **AO2**: insight into how Orwell *develops* our understanding of leadership across the whole novel, using characters as embodiments of different leadership qualities (structure).

[8] **AO3**: Allusions to two contexts – Orwell's 'snobbery' and the novel as an allegory – enriches the analysis in this answer.

[9] **AO1/AO3**: key concept – distinction between leaders and leadership – is strengthened by details of Orwell's personality and the political views he held.

Commentary

This answer is based on a perceptive inquiry into Orwell's intentions and a sensitive distinction between leaders and leadership. It explores this distinction and how it is revealed by Orwell's techniques such as characterisation, allusions to **symbolism** (for example, Boxer representing the 'stupid' working class) and vocabulary choices. The analysis is well-structured and supported effectively by references that are well-chosen and range widely across the text. Subject-specific terminology is relevant and useful and helps the answer to explore Orwell's deliberate choices. Contextual knowledge informs the analysis rather than being separate and pointless.

DO IT!

Now use what you have learned to answer the following AQA exam-style question.

How does Orwell use the character of Snowball in *Animal Farm* to explore ideas about leadership?

Write about:

- how Orwell presents Snowball
- how Orwell uses Snowball to explore ideas about leadership.

[30 marks]
AO4 [4 marks]

Question 5

'The most important lesson in *Animal Farm* is that trust is a very dangerous thing.'

How far do you agree with this statement?

Write about:

- examples of trust in the novel
- the consequences of trust in the novel.

[30 marks]
AO4 [4 marks]

Zoom in on the question

'The most important lesson in *Animal Farm* is that trust is a very dangerous thing.'

How far do you agree with this statement?

Write about:

- examples of trust in the novel
- the consequences of trust in the novel.

You don't have to agree completely that trust is the most important lesson but you need to be able to support your view. (AO1)

Keep to the question focus – (blind) trust and its (negative) consequences to address AO1.

Refer to the consequences of trust everywhere/Orwell's own experience of trusting leaders (for example, in Spain). (AO3)

Choose and explore some relevant details to support 'how far' you agree. (AO1/AO2)

Here are some ideas that could be included in an answer in order to cover the Assessment Objectives (AOs).

AO1	AO2	AO3
Discuss examples of trust in the novel and its consequences: Squealer's role in winning the trust, and subsequent oppression, of the animals; different sorts of trust and how these are represented by different animals, such as Boxer or the sheep.	Explore some examples of vocabulary choices at points when the pigs demand 'trust' and the development of the idea of trust through the novel. Consider how Orwell turns trust against the animals in a process that is bitterly ironic (Napoleon's strength is that he 'trusts nobody').	Discuss the significance of the 'fairy story' form chosen by Orwell. How might Orwell's own views and experiences (fighting in the Spanish Civil War, knowledge of the Russian Revolution) have influenced his intentions?

A student has decided to focus on the dangers of *blind trust* and whether Orwell is warning against *all* trust. This is the plan they have made to answer the question.

Paragraph	Content		Timing
1	Intro – use the question prep to establish focus of answer, and introduce distinction between blind trust and earned trust.		9.40
2	How the pigs exploit trust to promote their own power/ how Squealer uses the idea of 'trust'.	Refer back to question focus sometimes. Question whether Orwell is against *all* trust in *all* circumstances.	9.43
3	Disastrous consequences of trust/Orwell's cruel irony.		9.56
4	Snowball as worthy of trust. Necessary checks on trust.		10.09
5	Conclusion – agree but with qualification – what did Orwell intend? (Refer to his known views.)		10.22

The essay plan above will meet these Assessment Objectives:

AO1 Read, understand and respond	Examine Orwell's intentions and the tone that points to his intentions. Explore the development ideas and effects of trust throughout the novel. Give examples of trust placed (by the animals) and abused (by the pigs). Give examples of language related to 'trust'.
AO2 Language, form and structure	Analyse the effects of the examples chosen. Consider how Orwell develops trust, and its effects within his theme.
AO3 Contexts	Explore how knowledge of Orwell's own views might help us to understand his intentions.

In *Animal Farm*, trust has disastrous consequences[1] for most animals. After the revolution, Orwell implies that the animals trust each other's good intentions in order to be able to concentrate on survival[2]. However, he shows how the pigs exploit this unconditional trust: Boxer blindly trusts the pigs, who work him until he drops and then send him to the knacker; similarly, the sheep adopt the pigs' **maxims** of 'two legs bad' or 'two legs better' without question, even if they are contradictory and of no benefit to themselves or the other animals. The main benefit of the animals' blind trust for Napoleon is that he can turn himself into a replacement Jones, with all the luxuries and privileges that humans previously enjoyed at the animals' expense. By contrast, Snowball earns trust but does not (on the whole) abuse it.

Once the animals have accepted the argument that the pigs are intelligent and that the revolution depends on intelligent planning if the return of the hated Jones is to be avoided, unscrupulous pigs can get away with anything. Squealer always insists Napoleon is trustworthy and that not trusting him risks the return of Jones[3]. Squealer frequently uses the word 'trust' to insinuate the idea of the pigs' trustworthiness[4] into the animals' minds. For example[5], when they are upset that Napoleon has banned debates, Squealer says he 'trusts' that the animals appreciate the self-sacrificial efforts Napoleon is making as a leader. When they hear of the cruelty to animals on other farms and want to take action, Squealer urges them to restrain themselves and to 'trust in Comrade Napoleon's strategy.' He justifies this call to trust by calling Napoleon 'comrade' to remind the animals that[6] Napoleon is one of them – an equal. Ironically[6], Squealer later praises Napoleon for 'trusting nobody'. By then the animals should have realised that it is not just people Napoleon does not trust – it is animals too[6], just as Stalin/Napoleon did not trust the Russian masses and sought to control and exploit them.

By the time the animals finally recognise the pigs' untrustworthiness, the consequences of the animals' blind trust[7] cannot be reversed: they have almost broken themselves in rebuilding the windmill, and many animals have been savagely slaughtered by Napoleon's dogs. They are now in danger of losing everything that they have made such huge sacrifices for. By the end of the novel[8], the animals 'did more work and received less food' than animals on human-led farms. This neat opposition of the words 'more' and 'less' ironically references what the animals have lost compared with what they could have gained if Snowball's aims had been supported: a cut in the working week and heating in their stalls. In other words, following Snowball would probably have lead to less work and more comfort[9]. Napoleon uses the animals' trust against them, driving them

---

[1] **AO1:** clear opening, using words from the question to ensure relevance, and summing up the whole answer.

[2] **AO1:** 'conceptual' approach – an alternative view of the role of trust.

[3] **AO2:** perceptive appreciation of the role of trust within the structure of the plot.

[4] **AO2:** Repetition **technique** explored for its significance ('to insinuate...').

[5] **AO1:** references well chosen and introduced to illustrate point.

[6] **AO1/AO2:** neat development of analysis of how Orwell presents truth and its role within the plot.

[7] **AO1:** use of words from the question re-focuses the answer to keep it relevant.

[8] **AO2:** neatly traces the development of the consequences of trust through the novel to its climax at the end (structure).

constantly into poverty in order to enrich himself – just as Jones always did. Orwell emphasises this ironic reversal by making Pilkington praise the importance of trust in welcoming Napoleon as one of the human farmers. Before his toast, Pilkington celebrates the end of 'mistrust' between the pigs and the humans. He links this 'mistrust' to a 'misunderstanding', thus cheapening the whole idea of 'trust' as though it is just a tactic, something trivial, rather than a solemn commitment[9].

9 **AO2**: sensitivity to language choices leads to deeper insights into Orwell's intentions.

So, is Orwell saying that trust is a bad thing? I don't think he can be[10] because even Snowball seems to believe in the division of labour between brain workers and muscle workers. All the pigs – including Snowball – spend the months before the rebellion teaching themselves to read and – presumably – working out the Seven Commandments. They keep all this secret from the other animals. However, the difference between Snowball and Napoleon is that Snowball earns his trust by leading from the front[11], as he does in the Battle of the Cowshed, sustaining wounds in leading and protecting the other animals. Also, Snowball respects the trust placed in the pigs by encouraging the animals to question and contest the pigs' decisions in the Sunday debates and in the various committees that he sets up.

10 **AO1**: perceptive inquiry into Orwell's intentions, based on appreciation of details in the text.

11 **AO1**: further development of idea that trust is not necessarily dangerous.

Overall, I agree that the novel suggests that 'trust is a dangerous thing'. Perhaps Orwell is suggesting trust is necessary as long as it operates within democracy – Snowball's model of democracy. After all, Orwell always called himself a 'democratic socialist', and trust is a mark of the decency that Orwell always called for[12].

12 **AO1/AO3**: reference to relevant aspects of Orwell's own views and values helps us to understand his intentions.

Commentary

This is a thoughtful, enquiring response based on subtle distinctions between different sorts of trust and a sensitivity to Orwell's own likely intentions. This conceptualised approach is supported by a range of precise references that draw upon details across the text. The answer thus focuses on how Orwell uses the structure of the whole text to shape the reader's reactions. The answer includes subtle insights into the connotations of Orwell's language choices. Subject-specific terminology (for example, 'ironic', 'reversal', 'insinuate') is used precisely to highlight Orwell's intentions.

DO IT!

Now use what you have learned to answer the following AQA exam-style question.

'*Animal Farm* shows that greed is the most powerful force in society.'

How far do you agree with this statement?

Write about:

*   examples of greed in the novel
*   the power of greed in the novel.

[30 marks]
AO4 [4 marks]

Question 6

How far do you agree that Orwell creates 'a pessimistic view of human nature' in *Animal Farm*?

Write about:

- the view of human nature that Orwell presents in the novel
- how Orwell presents this view of human nature by the way he writes.

[30 marks]
AO4 [4 marks]

Zoom in on the question

How far do you agree that Orwell creates 'a pessimistic view of human nature' in *Animal Farm*?

Write about:

- what view of human nature Orwell presents in the novel
- how Orwell presents this view of human nature by the way he writes.

Explore Orwell's deliberate methods (language, structure) through which he influences the reader. (AO2)

Focus on the question – Orwell's view of human nature – to address AO1.

Give your own personal view based on evidence; this may be agreeing/disagreeing to some extent. (AO1)

Discuss views on 'human nature' held by people generally. What is 'human nature'? (AO3)

Here are some ideas that could be included in an answer in order to cover the Assessment Objectives (AOs).

AO1	AO2	AO3
Analyse how Orwell builds the reader's reaction to the corruption of the revolution. Consider the pigs as **symbols** of greed in humans. Refer to key events and Orwell's choice of language.	Analyse effects on the reader of Orwell's language and structure, for example, how the momentum of the plot makes the animals' fate/the pigs' triumph seem inevitable and depressing.	Consider the concept of 'human nature' and how typical assumptions about it might be reflected in Orwell's ideas and in the novel's events.

A student has decided to focus on how Orwell is very pessimistic. This is the plan they have made to answer the question.

Paragraph	Content		Timing
1	Intro – agree that Orwell is pessimistic.		1.30
2	How Orwell's view of human nature is in line with commonly held negative views about it – that people are largely greedy or stupid, like the animals.	Refer back to question focus sometimes. Consider how the plot is organised around relentless and worsening disasters, and how Orwell uses allegory to teach us a lesson.	1.33
3	Orwell's pessimism and how he mocks the naive, stupid animals (**dramatic irony** of blowing up windmill).		1.46
4	Circular structure of novel mocks Major's idealism.		2.00
5	Conclusion – summarise Orwell's attitude.		2.12

The essay plan above will meet these Assessment Objectives:

AO1 Read, understand and respond	Give a personal response to the topic, recognising that the novel has a strong purpose/message for us. Illustrate Orwell's pessimistic view by analysing the sequence of events in the plot and the tone of language.
AO2 Language, form and structure	Analyse the effect of structure and how Orwell's presentation of events seems to mock the animals' efforts and trust. Consider the role of allegory.
AO3 Contexts	Set Orwell's views in the context of generally held views on human nature, and in the context of the Russian Revolution.

Animal Farm is not about animals at all. It is an allegory of human society and the tendency for power to concentrate in the hands of a tiny elite group**❶**. Here, the elite is represented by the pigs and their ferocious bodyguards – the dogs. The rest of the animals represent the mass of people – the working class – who are exploited and oppressed until they rebel and overthrow their oppressors in a revolution. In the novel, Orwell is deeply pessimistic**❷** about the chances of success of a revolution. He shows how the leaders of the revolution become just as greedy, selfish and oppressive as the rulers who were overthrown. Worse than that, the novel seems to show this depressing process as completely inevitable, as though rebellion is completely pointless because it will be defeated by the workings of human nature.

Even the example of virtuous leadership (Snowball) offers no hope. Firstly, he is too naive to prepare to defend himself against Napoleon's savagery and, secondly, even he shows a tendency towards giving privileges to his own kind. For example**❸**, although the animals assume that in this new era of freedom and equality all animals will share the windfall apples, they are all taken by the pigs and even Snowball condones this.

Orwell's pessimistic presentation of human nature fits with views commonly held by pessimistic people in real life. People often wearily accept their lot with a shrug of 'What can you do? That's just human nature', which perhaps explains why many people around the world choose not to vote in elections, and even, in part, the presence of oppressive regimes throughout history**❹**. This attitude might well make Orwell's message of acceptance and helplessness more familiar and acceptable, and he never gives any hope to the reader that Napoleon's greed and wickedness will be checked – even Benjamin (representing the intellectuals), who quickly recognises that Napoleon's leadership is no better than that of Jones, is too cynical, or accepting, to take action. The rest of the animals' misery and poverty gets worse and worse, as each of the commandments (the basis of a fair society under Animalism) is undone**❺**, and when they get a chance to turn on the pigs, even Boxer, a model of honesty and goodness, absurdly blames himself for not working hard enough. The plot of *Animal Farm* gives no relief to this sense of the animals' headlong collapse into misery and degradation, a collapse explained by the basic failings of human nature – either selfishness (the pigs) or stupidity (the other animals)**❻**.

The corruption of the revolution in the novel seems unstoppable**❺**, perhaps reflecting Orwell's pessimistic views relating to revolution and change, for example in Russia**❶**. This pessimism is demonstrated when the windmill is rebuilt and the animals are proud that 'nothing short of explosives'**❻**

❶ AO1/AO3: understanding of the central idea in the task, linked to context of literary form – allegory.

❷ AO1: clear focus on task. The opening usefully explains how animals can shed light on *human* nature.

❸ AO1: well-chosen indirect references to support points.

❹ AO1/AO3: Orwell's views helpfully put in context of ideas generally held by people.

❺ AO2: insights into relentless plot structure and how this reinforces sense of pessimism.

❻ AO1/AO2: deft choice of structural feature coupled with useful comments on Orwell's deliberate effect on reader.

could destroy it. It is only a few pages later, unanticipated by any animal except the perceptive Benjamin, that the humans blow the windmill up, and Squealer claims this as a victory! Orwell uses dramatic irony to convey his bleak view. As the novel goes on, the reader knows what the pigs' real objectives and tactics are, but the animals do not. The windmill (which may be seen as a symbol of industrialisation in Russia) should benefit everyone and so offers hope, which is smashed. Even when the windmill is eventually successfully built, it is only the pigs (or the ruling classes in Russia) whose lives become easier as a result.

Orwell's pessimistic view is powerfully expressed by the structure of the novel: in the beginning, there is optimism, with Major's wonderful vision of freedom and the liberating of the animals' (humans') real potential; the ending closes a circle in which that vision is corrupted and turned on its head by the selfish and greedy pigs. It is the human greed and savagery represented by the pigs that triumphs, not the enlightenment and democracy represented by Major's vision. The novel's circular structure and its relentless plot of misery and betrayal make Orwell's message quite clear[7]: human nature is dominated either by cynical meanness or, perhaps worse, naive stupidity[8].

[7] **AO2**: precise commentary on how Orwell's pessimism is coded into the novel's 'circular structure'.

[8] **AO1**: Neat, incisive summary of Orwell's view.

Commentary

This is a vigorous and well-argued analysis of Orwell's pessimistic outlook. The student has used varied references to support their interpretation of Orwell's view of human nature. There is a clear and perceptive understanding of how literary (allegory) and social contexts interplay with Orwell's presentation. The answer usefully draws on subject-specific terminology (for example, 'allegory', 'represent') to support an exploration of how Orwell influences the reader. The comments on structural development and characterisation are precise and often profound.

DO IT!

Now use what you have learned to answer the following AQA exam-style question.

How far do you agree that in *Animal Farm* Orwell creates an important warning about the abuse of power?

Write about:

- the view of power and its abuse that Orwell presents in the novel
- how Orwell presents this power by the way he writes.

[30 marks]
AO4 [4 marks]

Orwell gave *Animal Farm* the subtitle, 'A Fairy Story'.

In what ways is 'A Fairy Story' a fitting subtitle for the novel?

Write about:

- ways in which *Animal Farm* is like a fairy story

- how Orwell uses fairy-story elements to support his themes.

[30 marks]
AO4 [4 marks]

Zoom in on the question

Orwell gave *Animal Farm* the subtitle, 'A Fairy Story'.

In what ways is 'A Fairy Story' a fitting subtitle for the novel?

Write about:

- ways in which *Animal Farm* is like a fairy story

- how Orwell uses fairy-story elements to support his themes.

Stay relevant to the focus of the exam question (fairy-story form) to address AO1.

Show your knowledge of relevant aspects of traditional fairy tales. (AO3)

Refer to key elements in fairy stories and explore how Orwell uses these to express his ideas. (AO1/AO2)

Analyse the effects of his use of specific fairy-story elements. (AO2/AO3)

Here are some ideas that could be included in an answer so as to cover the Assessment Objectives (AOs).

AO1
Explore how the novel is an allegory of how power and inequality developed in Russia after the Revolution.

AO2
Consider the plot as a means to lead to a 'lesson' for the reader (structure). Analyse the effects of Orwell's typical language style, and of some fairy-story elements.

AO3
Identify typical fairy-story elements and how these help Orwell's theme (eg animals, allegory/message, simple language).

A student has decided to focus on how the fairy story suits Orwell's purposes in some ways but not others. This is the plan they have made to answer the question.

Paragraph	Content		Timing
1	Intro – outline typical fairy-story characteristics and why Orwell might have used the FS form. Key idea: it makes the reader 'drop their guard', but is not always apt.		1.30
2	Animals as 'types', and the implications of these stereotypes.	Refer back to question focus sometimes. Question Orwell's implied views/assumptions.	1.33
3	Simple language style; how the pigs exploit simple language for their own ends.		1.46
4	'Dark' fairy story; how Orwell subverts the normal good vs evil aspect of a FS.		2.00
5	Conclusion – brief return to question; criticise Orwell's possibly patronising view implied in FS form.		2.12

The essay plan above will meet these Assessment Objectives:

AO1 Read, understand and respond	Examine and criticise Orwell's intentions/the implications of how he presents the animals' fate.
AO2 Language, form and structure	Discuss the use of fairy-story form and conventions to support Orwell's message. Consider the effects of Orwell's 'simple' style.
AO3 Contexts	Explore the significance of Orwell's explicit use of fairy-story conventions.

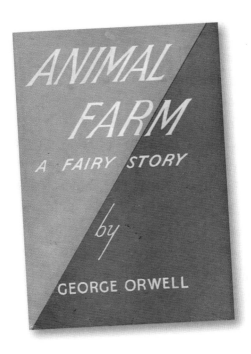

Traditional fairy stories[1], or 'fairy tales', have simple plots and simple characters – which are often animals. Despite this surface simplicity, the stories usually teach an important lesson about morality or human nature. They are often parables or allegories – stories whose simplicity hides their serious purpose. Orwell created *Animal Farm* along these lines – a story that seems very simple and even childish, but is in fact an allegory of something far more serious: in this case, the abuse of power and the failure of the Russian Revolution to stick to its original aim of freeing the masses from the oppression they had suffered for centuries. This is a big and controversial topic. The fairy-story form makes the reader drop their guard long enough for Orwell to convey his ideas[2].

As is typical of fairy stories[3] Orwell uses animals to represent human types, and he draws on how certain animals tend to be linked to particular stereotypes in fairy tales. For example, Boxer is introduced as 'an enormous beast'[4], which suggests that he is not very clever or sophisticated. He is praised for his 'great muscles'[4], implying that these are his main asset, rather than intellect. He is also slow-witted, a characteristic that Orwell confirms by making Boxer unable to learn the alphabet beyond the letter D[4]. In other words, Boxer fits the traditional **stereotype** of the cart horse – strong, faithful and dim. All the animals are presented in simple stereotyped ways: the cat is crafty, lazy and pleasure-seeking; the donkey is stubborn and hard to please, and so on[4]. The trouble with all these traditional stereotypes is that they are not always helpful. Orwell's animals are NOT equal – some are more intelligent and capable than others, with the implication that this is a natural state of affairs. Since the animals represent the working masses in a revolution, then perhaps Orwell is suggesting that some *people* are more deserving than others[5].

The simple, stereotyped characters[3] are matched by Orwell's use of the simple language typical of fairy stories. This makes *Animal Farm* very easy to read, even though it is an allegory of the fate of something as complex as the Russian Revolution. The fairy-story format allows Orwell to keep his political points remarkably simple and clear. Ironically, simple language is what makes the animals' new democracy very vulnerable to the pigs' distortions and manipulations. For example, Major's rich philosophy of 'Animalism' is reduced by the pigs to seven commandments so that all animals can understand it. The trouble with that simplification is that it makes it easy for the pigs to alter the commandments so that they work in their favour. For example, they allow themselves to sleep in beds simply by adding to the commandment 'No animal shall sleep in a bed' the two

---

1 AO1: clear opening, using words from the question to focus the answer on the fairy-story aspect rather than the novel as a whole.

2 AO1/AO3: 'conceptual' approach – Orwell's use of fairy-story form to engage the reader with a huge topic.

3 AO1: paragraphs are well linked and sequenced to support a developing point of view.

4 AO1: well-chosen evidence – both quotations and indirect references – to illustrate points.

5 AO1: contradictions in Orwell's presentation precisely identified and argued through, leading to *critical insights*.

words, 'with sheets'. It is ironic that Orwell's simplification technique is a powerful tool in the hands of the pigs, who use it to obscure rather than reveal truths[6].

[6] AO2: deft understanding of the effect of typical fairy-story language and its impact on Orwell's message.

Fairy stories are often allegories, which are meant to teach us something. Through the events of the 'fairy tale' of *Animal Farm*, Orwell explores how[7] power and secret organisations corrupt good intentions. In most fairy stories, however, it is good that triumphs and the 'baddies' get their comeuppance (for example, the third little pig outwits and kills the wolf). In *Animal Farm*, however, Orwell has the greedy and cynical pigs achieving complete victory by the end of the novel. This is a very dark fairy story indeed. It suggests that evil inevitably wins, just as Orwell saw it rising, triumphant over the Russian workers' hopes of freedom as that revolution developed[8].

[7] AO1: using Orwell's name helps to emphasise the novel as a deliberate construct with definite aims.

It could be argued that Orwell's view of the workers is similar to the way in which the pigs view the other animals on *Animal Farm*. A fairy story is usually a moral or life lesson for children: perhaps Orwell considered it to be a suitable form for his message because he saw the mass of people as being as naive and silly as children[8] – as though, like the animals ruled by the pigs, they are easily exploited.

[8] AO3: knowledge of the fairy-story form allows a richer understanding of Orwell's intentions.

Commentary

This is a perceptive, well-informed and carefully developed answer that successfully adopts an exploratory and critical approach to the novel and Orwell's intentions. The answer draws on wide-ranging references – both direct and indirect – to support the interpretation of the ways Orwell adapts the fairy-story form to his purposes. Knowledge and understanding of the literary context of the novel (fairy-story traditions) enrich the analysis, giving rise to some sharp, critical insights into the novel's likely effect on the reader. Subject-specific terminology (for example, 'allegory', **'parable'**, 'stereotype') is used helpfully in support of these insights.

DO IT!

Now use what you have learned to answer the following AQA exam-style question.

Animal Farm is a 'novella' – a very short novel.

In what ways is the short length of *Animal Farm* fitting for Orwell's purposes?

Write about:

- ways in which the short length of *Animal Farm* affects the reader
- how the short length of *Animal Farm* supports Orwell's themes.

[30 marks]
AO4 [4 marks]

How far does Orwell present Snowball as a hero in *Animal Farm*?

Write about:

- what Snowball says and does that could be seen as heroic

- how Orwell presents Snowball by the way he writes.

[30 marks]
AO4 [4 marks]

Zoom in on the question

How far does Orwell present Snowball as a hero in *Animal Farm*?

Write about:

- what Snowball says and does that could be seen as heroic

- how Orwell presents Snowball by the way he writes.

Keep to the question focus – whether or not Snowball is heroic – to address AO1.

Show an understanding of the idea of hero and heroism. (AO3)

Consider both for and against the idea suggested – there is more than one side to the answer. (AO1)

To meet AO2, explore how Orwell's deliberate intentions are conveyed through his methods (for example, language, plot).

Here are some ideas that could be included in an answer in order to cover the Assessment Objectives (AOs).

AO1
Outline Snowball's most prominent characteristics, including details of what he says and if that shows him to be a hero – or not. Consider non-heroic aspects of Snowball. Is he corrupted at all – like the other pigs – by the opportunity for privilege?

AO2
Explore how the course of events, Snowball's words (which both encourage and caution) and descriptions of him (for example, 'bloody streaks' for wounds) make us react to him. How trustworthy does Orwell imply him to be? What do we think about Snowball's absence from more than half of the novel?

AO3
Compare Snowball with conventional characteristics of a hero, including ideas of being a saviour, leadership and self-sacrifice.

A student has decided to focus on Orwell's negative presentation of heroes and heroism. This is the plan they have made to answer the question.

Paragraph	Content		Timing
1	Intro – use the question prep to establish focus of answer, and key idea of the *failure* of heroism to save the revolution from the pigs and humans.		1.30
2	Snowball's heroic qualities.	Refer back to question focus sometimes. Question how convincing a hero Snowball is.	1.33
3	The realistic, ordinary side of Snowball.		1.46
4	How Orwell makes us *feel* about Snowball. Look at some details (such as how Snowball is described/what he does) to infer Orwell's attitude (presentation).		2.00
5	Conclusion – brief return to question. How Snowball falls short of the common contemporary understandings of heroes – Jesus, Robin Hood, etc.		2.12

The essay plan above will meet these Assessment Objectives:

AO1 Read, understand and respond	Provide systematic analysis of Snowball's heroic (and non-heroic) qualities, and consider Orwell's intentions. Include relevant details to support the analysis.
AO2 Language, form and structure	Analyse details (for example, of language) to infer Orwell's tone and attitude.
AO3 Contexts	Explore Orwell's presentation of Snowball set in the wider context of heroes in society and literature.

Heroes in religion, literature and mythology are traditionally leaders AND saviours: if they are banished (for example Jesus, Moses, Robin Hood), they come back to inspire their followers and give them the hope they need to overthrow their oppressors, ensuring that goodness triumphs in the end[1]. By that definition, there are no heroes in *Animal Farm* because, at the end, the pigs have completely triumphed and their only two possible opponents – Snowball and Boxer – have been defeated. One has disappeared and the other is dead. Orwell leaves the animals with no hope of rescue from their fate; there is no hero to help them[2].

Early in the novel, Orwell does present Snowball with heroic qualities: most notably, he inspires and leads the animals to victory[3]. After the rebellion, he gives the animals hope by promising them a better life[3], in which slavery and being worked to death are no longer the purpose of living. He also upholds Major's vision and principles. It is Snowball who paints the Seven Commandments[3] on the wall so as to ensure that the true purpose of the revolution is always stuck to by the animals and their leaders. By including the detail that Snowball misspells some of the words, Orwell makes Snowball imperfect and more ordinary. This makes him both heroic AND one of the animals – not above them. At this point, his ordinariness emphasises his honesty, an important characteristic for a hero[4]. The most conventionally heroic thing about Snowball is that he leads in battle: he is 'at the head' of the main attack on the human invaders. In the final attack, Snowball is wounded in the charge but he keeps attacking, 'without halting for an instant'. Orwell makes it quite obvious that Snowball is heroically prepared to risk his own life for the cause and for his comrades[5].

However, Orwell emphasises that the risks Snowball takes in battle are calculated ones[6]. They are part of his carefully thought-out tactics that involve waves of defence and surprise counter-attacks, tactics he has learned from a study of Julius Caesar's command of the Roman army[6]. This means that every animal has a 'post' to go to. Orwell's use of the passive voice in saying that 'all preparations had been made' makes these preparations sound even more formal and deliberate, emphasising that the defence of the farm is not just spontaneous and passionate[7]. Certainly Snowball IS passionate about the animals' cause, but he is honest with them, even when that means disappointing them. For example, he tells Mollie that after the revolution there will be none of the sugar and ribbons that she values so much. So, overall, Orwell presents Snowball as a hero who is also ordinary, practical and trustworthy[8].

[1] **AO1:** clear opening, using words from the question to ensure relevance.

[2] **AO1/AO3:** 'conceptual' approach – question focus viewed in context of Orwell's attitude to heroism.

[3] **AO1:** deft choices of details to support points.

[4] **AO1/ AO2:** Orwell's intentions explored by considering the significance of how he presents a detail.

[5] **AO1/AO2:** apt quotations explored for their significance ('Orwell makes it quite obvious that…').

[6] **AO1:** development of analysis of how Orwell presents Snowball is well-supported by examination of details in the text.

[7] **AO2:** perceptive insight into significance of Orwell's language choices (syntax).

[8] **AO1:** excellent summary of the argument so far. Relevance to the question is re-secured.

However[9], how does Orwell[10] make us FEEL about Snowball? Is he completely trustworthy? If he had not been banished from the farm would he have remained a true 'animalist'? He is, after all, one of the pigs. There are hints right from the start that Snowball is less than heroic. Orwell[10] introduces him as 'quicker in speech and more inventive' than Napoleon, but clever talk and inventiveness are what the pigs rely on to fool and enslave their fellow animals. Orwell[10] also mentions that Snowball is considered to have not much 'depth of character', which seems to suggest that his heroic traits (bravery, integrity, leadership) are superficial. Orwell confirms this by having Snowball never return to the farm once he has been banished[11].

Rather than leading the animals to final victory, Snowball disappears suddenly and never returns. He doesn't come back to withstand further suffering for the cause. He is quite different from other great heroes contemporary readers would have known, such as Moses, Odysseus or Aslan. Orwell must have known what his readers typically would have expected of heroes, so he presumably deliberately chose not to make Snowball completely heroic[12]. Perhaps he is suggesting that heroes cannot be saviours: people have to save themselves.

[9] **AO1:** 'However' deftly signals another side to the argument.

[10] **AO1:** regular use of the author's name helps the answer to focus on Orwell's intentions, his views and how he tries to influence the reader.

[11] **AO1:** investigation of Orwell's intentions well-supported by consideration of details drawn from across the text.

[12] **AO3:** profound understanding of the concept of heroism in culture, at the time Orwell was writing, enriches our understanding of Orwell's message.

Commentary

This is a very profound answer that draws upon a perceptive understanding of the concept of heroism and how this is reflected in the literature and the religious ideas that would have been familiar to Orwell and his readership. The answer also includes a sharp analysis of the novel and details drawn from across the text. As a result, the answer is able to engage with both Orwell's attitude towards heroes and heroism, and with the unconscious assumptions about the topic that Orwell carried with him. Vocabulary used (for example, 'heroic qualities', 'saviour') is precise and supports a perceptive analysis of Orwell's ideas and assumptions.

DO IT!

Now use what you have learned to answer the following AQA exam-style question.

How far does Orwell present Squealer as evil in *Animal Farm*?

Write about:

- what Squealer says and does that could be seen as evil
- how Orwell presents Squealer.

[30 marks]
AO4 [4 marks]

Exam-style question 1

'The ending of *Animal Farm* suggests that attempts to achieve freedom are bound to fail.'

How far do you agree with this statement?

Write about:

- what happens towards the end of the novel
- how Orwell presents the ending.

[30 marks]
AO4 [4 marks]

PLANIT!

Answer steps	Content	Key ideas to refer to throughout answer	Minutes per step
Intro/Overall main point			
Sub-point 1			
Sub-point 2			
Sub-point 3			
Conclusion			

Exam-style question 2

Squealer says that leadership 'is a deep and heavy responsibility' for Napoleon.

How does Orwell use the character of Napoleon to explore ideas about leadership in *Animal Farm*?

Write about:

* what Napoleon says and does and what happens to him
* how Orwell presents different forms of leadership.

[30 marks]
AO4 [4 marks]

PLANIT!

Answer steps	Content	Key ideas to refer to throughout answer	Minutes per step
Intro/Overall main point			
Sub-point 1			
Sub-point 2			
Sub-point 3			
Conclusion			

Exam-style question 3

What ideas about power does Orwell explore in *Animal Farm*?

Write about:

- how Orwell uses different examples of power
- how Orwell presents these ideas by the way he writes.

[30 marks]
AO4 [4 marks]

PLANIT!

Answer steps	Content	Key ideas to refer to throughout answer	Minutes per step
Intro/Overall main point			
Sub-point 1			
Sub-point 2			
Sub-point 3			
Conclusion			

Exam-style question 4

How far does Orwell present Squealer as a dishonest character in *Animal Farm*?

Write about:

- what Squealer says and does that could be seen as dishonest
- how Orwell uses Squealer to explore the idea of dishonesty.

[30 marks]
AO4 [4 marks]

PLANIT!

Answer steps	Content	Key ideas to refer to throughout answer	Minutes per step
Intro/Overall main point			
Sub-point 1			
Sub-point 2			
Sub-point 3			
Conclusion			

How does Orwell present the influence of propaganda on the lives of the animals in *Animal Farm*?

Write about:

- the different sorts of propaganda and the effects of each in the novel
- how Orwell presents the influence of propaganda.

[30 marks]
AO4 [4 marks]

PLANIT!

Answer steps	Content	Key ideas to refer to throughout answer	Minutes per step
Intro/Overall main point			
Sub-point 1			
Sub-point 2			
Sub-point 3			
Conclusion			

Exam-style question 6

'It is strange that the animals do not rebel against the pigs in the same way they rebelled against Mr Jones.'

How far do you agree with this view of *Animal Farm*?

Write about:

- some of the events in the book

- how Orwell uses the animals to explore ideas about rebellion.

[30 marks]
AO4 [4 marks]

PLANIT!

Answer steps	Content	Key ideas to refer to throughout answer	Minutes per step
Intro/Overall main point			
Sub-point 1			
Sub-point 2			
Sub-point 3			
Conclusion			

Exam-style question 7

How far do you agree that Orwell creates 'a nightmarish vision of society' in *Animal Farm*?

Write about:

- the kind of society Orwell presents in the novel
- how Orwell presents this society.

[30 marks]
AO4 [4 marks]

PLANIT!

Answer steps	Content	Key ideas to refer to throughout answer	Minutes per step
Intro/Overall main point			
Sub-point 1			
Sub-point 2			
Sub-point 3			
Conclusion			

Exam-style question 8

How does Orwell use the relationships Napoleon has with the other animals to explore the idea of control in *Animal Farm*?

Write about:

- the different relationships Napoleon has with the other animals
- how Orwell uses these relationships to explore the idea of control.

[30 marks]
AO4 [4 marks]

PLANIT!

Answer steps	Content	Key ideas to refer to throughout answer	Minutes per step
Intro/Overall main point			
Sub-point 1			
Sub-point 2			
Sub-point 3			
Conclusion			

Glossary

adjective A word that describes a noun (for example: *tame* raven; *enormous* beast).

allegory A fictional story that has a moral message.

character A person/animal with human attributes in a novel created by the writer (for example: Napoleon, Mr Jones, Moses).

characteristic The words or actions a writer gives a **character**.

context The circumstances in which a novel is written or is read. For *Animal Farm*, these could include normal beliefs in 1945 about government or propaganda.

cyclical structure (circular plot) A storyline that ends at the same place or point that it begins. See **structure**.

dramatic irony This is when the reader knows something the characters do not. See **irony**, **situational irony** and **verbal irony**.

effect The impact that a writer's or **character's** words have on the reader; the mood, feeling or reaction the words create in the reader.

euphemism Giving something a milder name than it justifies, for example, 'fell asleep' instead of 'died', 'slender' rather than 'thin'. Euphemism is often used to soften bad news.

foreshadow A clue or a warning about a future event.

irony (ironic) 1 Mild sarcasm. A technique sometimes used by writers to mock a **character** and make them appear ridiculous or dishonest. **2** An event or result that seems to be the opposite of what could reasonably be expected. This causes a sort of bitter amusement to the victim (for example, it is ironic in *Animal Farm* that the pigs end up drinking alcohol – one of the principles of Animalism is that 'No animal shall drink alcohol.').

metaphor (metaphorically) Comparing two things by referring to them as though they are the same thing. (For example, when Moses talks of Sugar Candy Mountain, the clouds could be seen as a metaphor for the struggles the animals need to go through in order to reach the afterlife.)

parable A story designed to teach a lesson. For example, the parable of the Good Samaritan illustrates the importance of helping others – even enemies – when they are vulnerable.

phrase A group of words within a sentence.

propaganda Information (or mis-information) chosen to promote a particular point of view. For example, Squealer's propaganda is designed to serve the interests of the pigs.

represent To 'stand for' something. A symbol represents something. For example, Orwell chose the name Snowball as a symbol, knowing it would represent certain **characteristics** in the reader's mind.

stereotype A fixed set of assumptions that might be made about a whole category of people. For example, to assume that women are weak and over-emotional is a stereotype. Stereotypes are usually negative and are based on prejudices rather than reality.

structure (structurally) The way in which the events in a novel are ordered (for example, *Animal Farm* is arranged in ten chapters and uses a **cyclical structure**).

subject-specific terminology The technical or special terms used in a particular subject.

symbol (symbolic, symbolism) A symbol is something that represents something else. Using symbols can be a way for the author to influence a reader without them realising.

technique Another word for method. Writers use different techniques to create different **effects**.

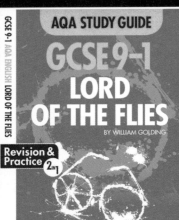

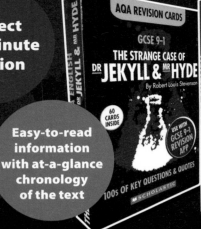

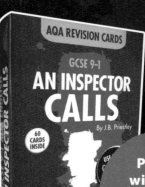